and Wisdom
of Women:
A Thought Book

by

Margaret Neylon

Attic Press
Dublin

First published by Attic Press, 1990

British Library Cataloguing in Publication Data
The Wit and wisdom of women : a thought book.
   1. Quoatations. Women writers
   I. Neylon, Margaret
   080

ISBN 1-85594-010-8

Cover Design: Luly Mason
Origination: Attic Press
Printing: Norhaven

MARGARET NEYLON lives in Dublin where she is Creative Director of an advertising agency. A short story writer and playwright, much of her work has been produced on radio.

Compiling the keywords alphabetically
I noticed that Sisterhood is followed
by Success and then Survival.
Is this a case of art imitating life?

Margaret Neylon

Their conversation is like a gently
wicked dance; sound meets
sound, curtsies, shimmies, and retires.
Another sound enters but
is upstaged by still another: the two
circle each other and stop.
Sometimes their words move in lofty
spirals: other times they
take strident leaps, and all of it is
punctuated with warm-pulsed
laughter...

Toni Morrison

The Wit and Wisdom of Women

A

Ability

Ability is sexless.

Christabel Pankhurst 20th Century

Action

If you want a thing well done, get a couple of old broads to do it.

Bette Davis 20th Century

When action grows unprofitable, gather information; when information grows unprofitable, sleep.

Ursula K Le Guin Contemporary

How beautiful it is to do nothing, and then rest afterwards.

Spanish Proverb

Activity

In a word, I am always busy, which is perhaps the chief reason why I am always well.

Elizabeth Cady Stanton 19th Century

Millions long for immortality who do not know what to do with themselves on a rainy Sunday afternoon.

Susan Ertz 20th Century

Adventure

That's why we become witches: to show our scorn of pretending life's a safe business, to satisfy our passion for adventure [...] to have a life of one's own, not an existence doled out to you by others.

Sylvia Townsend Warner 19/20th Century

Advice

I give myself sometimes admirable advice, but I am incapable of taking it.

Mary Wortley Montague 18th Century

The true secret of giving advice, is after you have honestly given it, to be perfectly indifferent whether it is taken or not and never persist in trying to set people right.

Hannah Whitall Smith 20th Century

Advice is what we ask for when we already know the answer but wish we didn't.

Erica Jong Contemporary

Age

You just wake up one morning, and you got it.

Moms Mabley 20th Century

Old age is not an illness, it is a timeless ascent. As power diminishes, we grow towards the light.

May Sarton Contemporary

When I am an old woman I shall
                              wear purple
With a red hat which doesn't go,
                    and doesn't suit me.
And I shall spend my pension on
                brandy and summer gloves
And satin sandals and say we've
                    no money for butter.

Jenny Joseph Contemporary

The great thing about getting older is that you don't lose all the other ages you've been.

Madeleine L'Engle 20th Century

As we reach midlife in the middle thirties or early forties, we are not prepared for the idea that time can run out on us, or for the startling truth that if we don't hurry to pursue our own definition of a meaningful existence, life can become a repetition of trivial maintenance duties.

Gail Sheehy Contemporary

Anger

Anger as soon as fed is dead
'Tis starving makes it fat.

Emily Dickinson 19th Century

Bitterness is like cancer. It eats upon the host. But anger is like fire. It burns it all clean.

Maya Angelou Contemporary

Anxiety

How often, while women and girls sit
warm at a snug fireside, their hearts and
imagination are doomed to divorce
from the comfort surrounding their
persons, forced out by night to wander
through dark ways, to dare stress of
weather, to contend with the snowblast,
to wait at lonely gates and stiles in
wildest storms, watching and listening
to see and hear the father, the son, the
husband coming home.

Charlotte Brontë 19th Century

Attitude

You've got to get up every morning
                    with a smile on your face,
And show the world all the love in your
                                            heart,
Then people gonna treat you better.
You're gonna find, yes, you will,
That you're beautiful as you feel.

Carole King Contemporary

B

Beauty

Adornment is never anything except a
reflection of the heart.

Coco Chanel 19/20th Century

The beauty of the world has two edges,
one of laughter, one of anguish, cutting
the heart asunder.

Virginia Woolf 20th Century

You can take no credit for beauty at
sixteen. But if you are beautiful at sixty,
it will be your soul's own doing.

Marie Stopes 19/20th Century

Beauties are always curious about
beauties, and wits about wits.

Maria Edgeworth 19th Century

If beauty is a letter of introduction -
wrinkles are a good résumé.

Mary Ellen Pickham 19/20th Century

Beauty endures only for as long as it can
be seen; goodness, beautiful today, will
remain so tomorrow.

Sappho 6th Century BC

Belief

Trust in God; she will provide.

Emmeline Pankhurst 19/20th Century

Why indeed must 'God' be a noun? Why
not a verb .. the most active and
dynamic of all?

Mary Daly Contemporary

God is love but get it in writing.

Gypsy Rose Lee 20th Century

The experience of God, or in any case the possibility of experiencing God, is innate.

Alice Walker Contemporary

Neither reproaches nor encouragements are able to revive a faith that is waning.

Nathalie Sarraute Contemporary

To keep a lamp burning we have to keep putting oil in it.

Mother Teresa Contemporary

The mob that would die for a belief seldom hesitates to inflict death upon any opposing heretical group.

Ellen Glasgow 20th Century

Opinions differ most when there is least scientific warrant for having any.

Daisy Bates 19th/20th Century

Books and Writing

Live merrily, little daughter-book, even if I cannot and we cannot; recite yourself to all who will listen; stay happy and wise. Wash your face and take your place without fuss in the Library of Congress for all books end up there eventually, both little and big [...] Do not get glum when you are no longer understood, little book. Do not curse your fate. Do not reach up from readers' laps and punch their noses, little book! For on that day, we will be free!

Joanna Russ Contemporary

I am, fundamentally, I think, an outsider. I do my best work and feel most braced with my back to the wall. It's an odd feeling, though, writing against the current: difficult entirely to disregard the current. Yet, of course, I shall.

Virginia Woolf 20th Century

The art of writing is the art of applying the seat of the pants to the seat of the chair.

Mary Heaton Vorse 20th Century

How am I to feel when discussed in the Harvard Guide of Contemporary American Literature under the great lump *Women Writers*, the only works of mine analysed being those that deal explicitly with women's problems - the rest of my books ignored, as if they had never been written? Insult, hurt, anger, frustration, indifference, amusement? Or gratitude for being recognised at all, even if it is only as a woman writer?

Joyce Carol Oates Contemporary

Books, books, books. It was not that I read so much. I read and re-read the same ones. But all of them were necessary to me. Their presence, their smell, the letters of their titles, and the texture of their leather bindings.

Colette 20th Century

C

Celebration

You wrote me a lovely letter on my 90th
birthday. What I have done looks small
to me, but I have tried a good deal for
the best I have known [...] don't you
think that the best things in life are
already in view? The opportunities for
women, the growing toleration and
sympathy in religion, the sacred cause
of peace? I have lived like Moses, to see
the entrance into the Promised Land.
How much is this to be thankful for!

Julia Ward Howe, Letter to Mrs Spofford,
19th/20th Century

Change

The change of one simple behaviour can affect other behaviours and thus change many things.

Jean Baer 20th Century

Nobody told me how hard and lonely change is.

Joan Gilbertson Contemporary

People change and forget to tell each other.

Lillian Hellman 20th Century

If civilisation is to advance at all in the future, it must be through the help of women, women freed of their political shackles, women with full power to work their will in society.

Emmeline Pankhurst 19/20th Century

Change your life today. Don't gamble on the future, act now, without delay.

Simone de Beauvoir 20th Century

There is no subject on which I am more inclined to hold my peace and learn, than on the "Woman Question". It seems to me to overhang abysses, of which even prostitution is not the worst. Conclusions seem easy so long as we keep large blinkers on and look in the direction of our individual private path.

Mary Anne Evans (George Eliot) 19th Century

Character

Parents can only give good advice or put them on the right paths, but the final forming of a person's character lies in their own hands.

Anne Frank 20th Century

From a timid, shy girl I had become a woman of resolute character, who could no longer be freighted by the struggle with troubles.

Anna Dostoevsky 19/20th Century

Character contributes to beauty. It
fortifies a woman as her youth fades.

Jacqueline Bisset Contemporary

Children

My baby has no name yet
like an unnamed bluebird or white
flowers
from the farthest land for the first,
I have no name for this baby of ours.

Kim Nam Jo Contemporary

I got more children than I can rightly
take care of, but I ain't got more than I
can love.

Ossie Guffy 20th Century

If you have never been hated by your
child, you have never been a parent.

Bette Davis 20th Century

A child is fed with milk and praise.

Mary Lamb 19th Century

I love all of my children. Some of them I don't like.

Lilian Carter 20th Century

Choice

To gain that which is worth having, it may be necessary to lose everything else.

Bernadette Devlin McAliskey Contemporary

Whenever I have to choose between two evils, I always like to try the one I haven't tried before.

Mae West 20th Century

Comfort and Consolation

Everyone knows that you can't relieve an itch by stroking it gently.

Elaine Morgan 20th Century

Efua put her hand on my cheek: 'Sister, you have need of a sister-friend because

you need to weep, and you need
someone to watch you while you weep.'

Maya Angelou Contemporary

Where's a man could ease a heart like a
satin gown?

Dorothy Parker 20th Century

Communication

Some people talk simply because they
think sound is more manageable than
silence.

Margaret Halsey 20th Century

Once you find your voice you know that
you can never be passively silent again.
Your spur to creation is the desire to
communicate. To have a meaningful
exchange with other people in order to
develop yourself and therefore your
work even further. So much, yet so little
time? The only answer is DO IT NOW!

Maud Sulter Contemporary

Community

Whatever the core problem is for the people of a country, will also be the core problem addressed by women, consciously or otherwise. We do not exist in a vacuum. We are anchored in our own place and time and we are part of communities that interact.

Audre Lord Contemporary

Courage

Everyone has talent. What is rare is the courage to follow the talent to the dark place where it leads.

Erica Jong Contemporary

You love like a coward. Don't take no steps at all. Just stand around and hope for things to happen outright. Unthankful and unknowing like a hog under an acorn tree. Eating and grunting with your ears hanging over your eyes, and never even looking up to see where the acorns are coming from.

Zora Neale Hurston 20th Century

I was still going to school when I heard of this courageous Indian woman for the first time [...] I trembled with excitement: not alone for the white woman is it possible to attain an independent position, the brown Indian too can make herself free. For days I thought of her and I have never been able to forget her. See what one good example can do! It spreads its influence so far.

Raden Adjeng Kartini 19th Century

Remember, Ginger Rogers did everything Fred Astaire did, but she did it backwards and in high heels.

Faith Whittlesey 20th Century

Crazy

How do I know all this? Because I'm crazy. You can always trust the information given you by people who are crazy; they have an access to truth not available through regular channels.

Norma Jean Harris Contemporary

I thought every house had to have its crazy woman or crazy girl, every village its idiot. Who would it be at our house? Probably me [...] I was messy, my hair tangled and dusty, my dirty hands broke things [...] And there were adventurous people inside my head to whom I talked whenever I was frivolous, violent, orphaned.

Maxine Hong Kingston Contemporary

Creativity

Creative minds have always been known to survive any kind of bad training.

Anna Freud 20th Century

We are traditionally rather proud of ourselves for having slipped creative work in there between the domestic chores and obligations. I'm not sure we deserve such a big A-plus for all that.

Toni Morrison Contemporary

The art of being an artist, if you weren't born in the right place, is to be able to live through rejections. A lot of them. To be able to speak when silenced. To be able to hear when not being heard. To be able to see and make seen when no one looks.

Gabriela Müller Contemporary

When I thought what do I as a woman want to say right now about creativity, these words came: What I have wanted to be and what I am are not the same, ever. I know that the more honestly I accept and express what I am, and put it into relation with what I supposed was intended for my life, the more creative I am. Thus fantasy and reality are continually being set against each other.

Alix Pirani Contemporary

All artists, in whatever medium, in fact work largely through the feminine side of their personalities. This is because works of art are essentially formed and created inside the mind of the maker, and are hardly at all dependent on external circumstances.

Joan Riviere Contemporary

Custom and Tradition

In electing me chief among you, through a period fraught with grave issues [...] you have reverted to an old tradition, and restored Indian women to the classic epoch of our country's history.

Sarojini Naidu 19/20th Century

The young people settling in Switzerland would have to obey Swiss law and restrict themselves to one partner at a time. To me this seems unfair. It may suit a Tibetan peasant to have two or three husbands simultaneously, whereas a rich European woman may prefer to have two or three in rapid succession, but why should Tibetans be forced to conform to European standards?

Dervla Murphy Contemporary

D

Death

Death must be an evil - and the gods agree;
for why else would they live forever?

Sappho 6th Century BC

Drink and dance and laugh and lie,
Love, the reeling midnight through,
For tomorrow we shall die!
(But, alas, we never do.)

Dorothy Parker 20th Century

The mother of a friend of mine died the other day. My friend's 11-year old child was sent away until after the funeral. She must be spared the knowledge of death. Is this not characteristic of our society? We treat death as if it were an aberration. Age approaches but beauticians, masseurs, and gland specialists co-operate to keep alive the illusion that we are not really growing older. Anything that reminds us of the inescapable fact that we are to die seems morbid to us. Yet without the serene acceptance of death as inexorable we lose all the magic and wonder of life.

Dorothy Thompson 20th Century

Democracy

I think democracy takes time. The benefits are so high the voice of every woman counts, and counts equally, and even though it costs time and even though we have to cope with a little chaos sometimes because of it, it is worth it.

Sigmunden Kristansdottir Contemporary

Why we oppose votes for men [...]
because men are too emotional to vote.
Their conduct at baseball games and
political conventions shows this, while
their innate tendency to appeal to force
renders them particularly unfit for the
task of government.

Alice Duer Miller 19/20th Century

Desire and Passion

To be with you, my love,
is not at all like being in heaven
but like being in the earth.

Moya Cannon Contemporary

By the time you say you're his
Shivering and sighing
And he vows his passion is
Infinite, undying -
Lady, make a note of this
One of you is lying.

Dorothy Parker 20th Century

Helen could hardly restrain herself from saying out loud what she thought of a man who brought up his daughter so that at the age of 24 she scarcely knew that men desired women and was terrified by a kiss. 'You oughtn't to be frightened', she said, 'It is the most natural thing in the world. Men will want to kiss you, just as they will want to marry you. Pity is to get things out of proportion. It is like noticing the noises people make when they eat, or men spitting, or in short, any small thing that gets on one's nerves.

Virginia Woolf 20th Century

Difficulties

In the face of an obstacle which is impossible to overcome, stubbornness is stupid.

Simone de Beauvoir 20th Century

Difficulties, opposition, criticism - these things are meant to be overcome, and there is a special joy in facing them and in coming out on top. It is only when there is nothing but praise that life loses its charm, and I begin to wonder what I should do about it.

Vijaya Lakshmi Pandit 20th Century

Bad moments, like good ones, tend to be grouped together.

Edna O'Brien Contemporary

Problems are messages.

Shakti Gawain 20th Century

Dignity and Humanity

We dreamed that women might be taken to be so extremely human that one would know, even without laboratory evidence, that where a woman is diminished in her integrity, in her rights, humankind is diminished because of it.

Andrea Dworkin Contemporary

Certain older women in villages become very independent and respected. Christianity shook this attitude very badly; it was not considered nice or feminine to speak out. But the dignity which African woman has and which was lost through colonisation is coming back.

Buchi Emecheta Contemporary

I'll keep my personal dignity and pride to the very end - it's all I have left and it's a possession that only myself can part with.

Daisy Bates 19/20th Century

E

Earth

We are sitting together in this one boat,
the Earth, this planet, and anything that
has to be changed will have to be in
agreement between the North and the
South, and I insist on giving fairer terms
to the South than we have had.

Roshan Dhunjibhoy Contemporary

We are living beyond our means. As a
people we have developed a lifestyle
that is draining the Earth of its priceless
and irreplaceable resources without
regard for the future of our children and
people all around the world.

Margaret Mead 20th Century

They take paradise, put up a parking
lot.

Joni Mitchell Contemporary

Education

Life is my college. May I graduate well,
and earn some honours!

> *Louisa May Alcott 19th Century*

Did she drop out or was she pushed?

> *Anonymous Contemporary*

Men have had every advantage of
women in telling their own story.
Education has been theirs in so much
higher a degree: the pen has been in
their hands.

> *Jane Austen 18th Century*

Energy

Physical and mental energy come from
feeling in control of your life, having
real choices and being involved with
others to find ways of organising for a
change for the better.

> *Barbara Rogers Contemporary*

Equality

Women who want to be equal to men lack ambition.

Anonymous Contemporary

Men and women shall have equal rights throughout the United States and in every place subject to its jurisdiction.

Alice Paul, Equal Rights (Lucretia Mott) Amendment 1923

Equality of rights under the law shall not be denied or abridged by the United States or by any State on account of sex.

The Equal Rights Amendment, USA

It was only when they [the government officials] became convinced that they were going to be held politically accountable, ie votes, that is the only point at which these people were seriously interested in hearing what we had to say and that is the point at which we ended up sitting around the table with the top lawyers for the government negotiating the type of Equal Rights Amendment we felt was necessary.

Marilou McPhedran Contemporary

Women who are heads of households must respond to the government just as ordinary heads of households but because we are women we do not enjoy equal rights [...] the only equality I share with men who are heads of households is the onerous duty of paying taxes.

Kasunose Kita 19th Century

Eroticism

Erotic comes from the Greek word eros, the personification of love in all its aspects [...] and personifying creative power and harmony. When I speak of the erotic, then, I speak of it as an assertion of the life force of women, of that creative energy empowered, the knowledge and use of which we are

now reclaiming in our language, our
history, our dancing, our loving, our
work, our lives.

Audre Lord Contemporary

Exile

It's not me as an individual they are
sending into exile. They think that with
me they can also ban the political ideas
[...] I couldn't think of a greater honour.

Winnie Mandela Contemporary

Why are we waiting
Get me the DC. 9
New York, New World
New Suitcase, transit visa.

Leland Bardwell Contemporary

F

Fear

Fear has a smell, as love does.

Margaret Atwood Contemporary

Everything is so dangerous that nothing is really very frightening.

Gertrude Stein 19/20th Century

The liar in her terror wants to fill up the void with anything. Her lies are a denial of her fear: a way of maintaining control.

Adrienne Rich Contemporary

Only when one is no longer afraid to die is one no longer afraid at all. And only when we are no longer afraid do we

begin to live in every experience,
painful or joyous, to live in gratitude for
every moment, to live abundantly.

Dorothy Thompson 20th Century

Fear no more, says the heart. Fear no
more, says the heart, committing its
burden to some sea which sighs
collectively for all sorrows, and renews,
begins, collects, lets fall.

Virginia Woolf 20th Century

Feminism

I myself have never been able to find
out precisely what feminism is: I only
know that people call me a feminist
whenever I express sentiments that
differentiate me from a doormat.

Rebecca West 20th Century

My consciousness is fine. It's my pay
that needs raising.

Anonymous Contemporary

It was rapidly becoming clear in my mind that men regarded women as a servant class in the community, and that women were going to remain in the servant class until they lifted themselves out of it.

Emmeline Pankhurst 19/20th Century

Much male fear of feminism is the fear that, in becoming whole human beings, women will cease to mother men, to provide the breast, the lullaby, the continuous attention associated by the infant with the mother. Much male fear of feminism is infantilism - the longing to remain the mother's son, to possess a woman who exists purely for him.

Adrienne Rich Contemporary

Food and Drink

I refuse to believe that trading recipes is silly. Tuna fish casserole is at least as real as corporate stock.

Barbara Grizzuti Harrison Contemporary

One reason I don't drink is that I want to know when I am having a good time.

Nancy Astor 19/20th Century

Never eat anything at one sitting that you can't lift.

Miss Piggy

One cannot live well, love well or sleep well unless one has dined well.

Virginia Woolf 20th Century

Forgiveness

If you haven't forgiven yourself something, how can you forgive others?

Dolores Huerta Contemporary

Freedom

I Mabel Hampton have been a lesbian all my life, for 82 years, and I am proud of myself and my people. I would like all my people to be free in this country and all over the world, my gay people and my black people ...

Mabel Hampton 20th Century

What is the good of talking about the glorious past of India if you are living in slavery today? [...] Lovers of freedom all over the world ought to co-operate in freeing from slavery one-fifth of the human race. I call upon you to rise and salute the flag of Indian independence!

Bhikaiji Cama 19/20th Century

How is my own life-work serving to end these tyrannies, the corrosions of sacred possibility?

June Jordan Contemporary

The white fathers told us, 'I think therefore I am' and the Black mother within each of us - the poet - whispers in our dreams, I feel, therefore I can be free.

Audre Lord Contemporary

Learning moment by moment to be free in our minds and hearts, we make freedom possible for everyone the world over.

Sonia Johnson Contemporary

Who ever walked behind anyone to freedom? If we can't go hand in hand, I don't want to go.

Hazel Scott 20th Century

If civilisation is to advance at all in the future, it must be through the help of women, women freed of their political shackles, women with full power to work their will in society.

Emmeline Pankhurst 19/20th Century

Every day I express the ardent desire that women be freed from their subjection [...] I am ready to go to all lengths to achieve this aim. I hope that our two hundred million women do not turn their backs on their responsibilities as citizens. Hurry, hurry, women, save yourselves!

Jiu Jin 19th Century

We Make Freedom.

Women in South Africa Contemporary

Friendship

Friend derives from a word meaning 'free'. A friend is someone who allows us the space and freedom to be while relationships with lovers often feel binding.

Debbie Alicen 1983

And what a delight it is to make friends with someone you have despised!

Colette 19/20th Century

I have always made a distinction between my friends and my confidants. I enjoy the conversation of the former; from the latter I hide nothing.

Edith Piaf 20th Century

What can I do with the sea? Look at it. That is not enough for me. Swim? I do not like the horizontal position [...] I love the vertical, walking, climbing a mountain. I love the sense of power that results. Before the ocean I am a spectator: as if I were sitting in a box at

the theatre [...] besides that, the sea
either intimidates or makes one grow
soft. The sea resembles love too much. I
do not like love. (There is always the
question of sitting and waiting for what
love will do with me). I love friendship:
a mountain.

Marina Tsvetayeva 19/20th Century

Fun and Laughter

Put a little fun in your life - try dancing.

Kathryn Murray 20th Century

One loses many laughs by not laughing
at oneself.

Sara Jeannette Duncan Contemporary

When we begin to take our failures non-
seriously, it means we are ceasing to be
afraid of them. It is of immense
importance to learn to laugh at
ourselves.

Katherine Mansfield 19/20th Century

You grow up the day you have your first real laugh - at yourself.

Ethel Barrymore 20th Century

People that keep stiff upper lips find that it's damn hard to smile.

Judith Guest Contemporary

If I smiled or laughed, my helper did too. The universal language. This amazed me. I would have thought that tears were the things which bound us together, but no - smiles, laughter - and they warm up immediately. Understand my ridiculous self, thank you, yes. We are ridiculous, aren't we - black, white, yellow? If we cannot have some laughter we would crumble. Colour be damned. We must laugh together.

Katherine Hepburn Contemporary

The black child must learn early to allow laughter to fill his mouth, or the

million small cruelties he encounters
will congeal and clog his throat.

Maya Angelou Contemporary

Future

Keep in mind always the present you
are constructing. It should be the future
you want.

Alice Walker Contemporary

What is astonishing, what can give us
enormous hope and belief in a future in
which the lives of women and children
shall be amended and rewoven by
women's hands, is all that we have
managed to salvage, of ourselves, for
our children [...] the tenderness, the
passion, the trust in our instincts, the
evocation of a courage we did not know
we owned, the detailed apprehension of
another human existence, the full
realisation of the cost and
precariousness of life. The mother's
battle for her child - with sickness, with

poverty, with war, with all the forces of exploitation and callousness that cheapen human life - needs to become a common human battle, waged in love and in the passion for survival.

Adrienne Rich Contemporary

One of the things that is most striking about the young generation is that they never talk about their future, there are no futures for this generation, not any of them, and so naturally they never think of them. It is very striking, they do not live in the present, they just live, as well as they can, and they do not plan. It is extraordinary that whole populations have no projects for the future, none at all. It certainly is extraordinary, but it is certainly true.

Gertrude Stein 19/20th Century

The future is made of the same stuff as the present.

Simone Weil 20th Century

G

Goals

It is good to have an end to journey towards; but it is the journey that matters, in the end.

Ursula K Le Guin Contemporary

Growing Up

Why is it us girls are kept in when it's the boys who cause the trouble?

Poster Contemporary

I knew I would one day have those adult organs I saw in females around me and did not much care about. How could this be going to happen to me? I looked forward to savouring the sensation of difference with fierce curiosity [...] and how did I feel? Like a door opening on to my real self, on to a natural growth of generous giving, of loving [...] an expansion of soul and accompanying body.

Julia Strachey 20th Century

At school, at 14, a girl who considers you and your friends to be very fast, minces up to you all in the dinner hour, sniggering, and says, pursing her mouth up, 'I bet you're talking about rude things'. When you ask her what it is she means by 'rude things' she goes purple, stands on one leg, waggling the other, and finally explodes 'Boys!'

Eleanor Bron Contemporary

Guilt

I'm an Irish Catholic and I have a long iceberg of guilt.

Edna O'Brien Contemporary

It is scarcely possible that an English or Irish Protestant of the present day [...] can look back to the past history of Ireland, especially in connection with its terrible Penal Code, without a feeling of grief and of shame. The sleepless eyes of Justice have never ceased to watch throughout the long centuries of wrongs done to Ireland. We [English] are not personally responsible, but nationally we are deeply responsible.

Josephine Butler 19th Century

H

Habit

The only difference between a rut and a grave is their dimensions.

Ellen Glasgow 20th Century

Happiness

The Muses have made me happy
in my lifetime

and when I die
I shall never be forgotten.

Sappho 6th Century BC

Happiness is good health and a bad memory.

Ingrid Bergman 20th Century

Spring is here, and I could be very happy, except that I am broke.

Edna St Vincent Millay 19th Century

One is happy as a result of one's own efforts, once one knows the necessary ingredients of happiness - simple tastes, a certain degree of courage, self-denial to a point, love of work, and above all, a clear conscience. Happiness is no vague dream, of that I now feel certain.

George Sand (Amandine Aurore Lucie Dupin) 19th Century

When a small child [...] I thought that success spelled happiness. I was wrong, happiness is like a butterfly which appears and delights us for one brief moment, but soon flits away.

Anna Pavlova 19/20th Century

Home

She was back in Africa. And that felt
like fresh honey on the tongue: a
mixture of complete sweetness and
smokey roughage. Below was home
with its unavoidable warmth. Oh
Africa! Crazy continent.

Ama Ata Aidoo Contemporary

But everybody needs a home so at least
you can have some place to leave which
is where most other folks will say you
must be coming from.

June Jordan Contemporary

Hopes and dreams

Wanna fly, you have to give up the shit
that weighs you down.

Toni Morrison Contemporary

Now sometimes it can be a very dangerous thing to go in search of a dream, for the reality does not always match it.

Gracie Fields 20th Century

One can never consent to creep when one feels an impulse to soar.

Helen Keller 20th Century

People pretend not to like grapes when they are too high for them to reach.

Marguerite de Navarre 16th Century

Those who lose dreaming are lost.

Australian Aboriginal Proverb

Like Gothic fantasy, science-fiction opens up a universe of possibilities for women. If women's lives are restricted on Earth, then travelling heroinism takes us off Earth through time and space.

Sarah Lefanu Contemporary

In the Alps you can sometimes walk up thousands of feet in a reverie almost without noticing them, handing over the whole business of where to put your feet to automatic centres; a semi-dream, full of delicious memories of all the nicest things that ever happened, or equally beguiling visions of castles in Spain, floats you up. Rare and fortunate days these, for you reach the top of the slope and wake up, almost refreshed [...] Do you dream because you are walking so easily? Or do you walk so easily because you dream?

Dorothy Pilley 20th Century

Housework

There are days when housework seems the only outlet.

Adrienne Rich Contemporary

A slave is a person who is not paid for working. Sound familiar?

Astra Contemporary

Cleaning your house
While your kids are still growing
Is like shovelling the walk
Before it stops snowing.

Phyllis Diller 20th Century

Humour

Do you know the women's movement
has no sense of humour?
No, but if you'll hum a few bars I'll fake
it.

Anonymous Contemporary

Yo'ole black hide don't look lak nothin'
tuh me, but uh passel uh wrinkled up
rubber, wid yo' big ole yeahs flappin' on
each side lak uh paih uh bussard wings.

Zora Neale Hurston 20th Century

Let us enjoy the banana skin
bringing dictators to the ground.

Eithne Strong Contemporary

It was so cold the other day, I almost got married.

Shelly Winter Contemporary

I

Ideals

Those who serve a cause are not those who love that cause. They are those who love the life which has to be led in order to serve it [...] and they are rare.

Simone Weil 20th Century

I only want to ride the wind and walk the waves, slay the big whale of the Eastern Sea, clean up the frontiers and save the people from drowning. Why should I imitate others, bow my head, stoop over and be a slave? Why resign myself to menial housework?

Trieu Thi Trinh 2nd Century

I'd rather have roses on my table than
diamonds on my neck.

Emma Goldman 19/20th Century

No man or woman who tries to pursue
an ideal in his or her own way is
without enemies.

Daisy Bates 19/20th Century

Ideas

I had never been as resigned to ready-
made ideas as I was to ready-made
clothes, perhaps because, although I
couldn't sew, I could think.

Jane Rule Contemporary

Identity

black woman, of black people, glorying
in self and sisterhood,
in truth i am named womanist.

my name is many and in truth
without all parts i have no name at all,
for if we cannot name with love and
connectedness
how may we grow round and full with
the earth?

Adjoa Andoh Contemporary

Identity is what you can say you are
according to what they say you can be.

Jill Johnston Contemporary

I know I'm black, I see it all the time, I
like it. I wouldn't want to wash it off.

Joan Armatrading Contemporary

Am I fact? Or am I fiction? Am I what I
know I am? Or am I what he thinks I
am?

Angela Carter Contemporary

I do not want to be a wife [...] a mistress, yes, with a lover, yes of course, but not a wife. There is something in that word that does not suit me. As a wife I am never free. I am a shadow of myself.

Flora Nwapa Contemporary

Passes are identity documents.. A pass must be carried by all blacks over the age of sixteen [...] and a loss of a pass can turn a normally law-abiding person into one with a criminal record. Passes regulate the movement of millions of blacks. Every year nearly half a million people are imprisoned for pass offences alone. As a result it has become part and parcel of city life for a black to be in and out of jail. No longer is there any stigma attached to it. In fact, the opposite applies. A family in which no member has ever been imprisoned is highly suspect - they must surely have come to some arrangement with the police to report others in exchange for immunity!

Winnie Mandela Contemporary

Imperialism

Their bloody kings and their bloody
queens. Their bloody peers. Their
bloody generals, admirals, explorers.
Livingstone, Hillary, Kitchener. All the
bwanas. And all their beaters, porters,
sherpas. Who found the source of the
Nile, Victoria Falls. The tops of
mountains. Their so-called discoveries
reek of untruth. How many dark people
died so they could misname the
physical features in their blasted
gazeteer? A statistic we shall never
know. Dr Livingstone, I presume you
are here to rape our land and enslave
our people.

Michelle Cliff Contemporary

You read in the paper 'Campesinos
invade such and such a piece of land'.
That is not true. We do not invade land,
we recover land that belongs to us by
law, but was invaded by the big
landowners or the foreign companies.

Elvia Alvarado Contemporary

Independence

How much bondage and suffering a woman escapes when she takes the liberty of being her own physician of both body and soul.

Elizabeth Cady Stanton 19th Century

I am told I must modestly cast down my eyes. I will not do that. I will look at men, as well as women, straight in the eye, not cast down my own before them.

Raden Adjeng Kartini 19th Century

If you don't like my ocean
Don't fish in my sea
Stay out of my valley
And let my mountains be!

Ma Rainey Contemporary

Injustice

Since when do you have to agree with people to defend them from injustice?

Lillian Hellman 20th Century

Women constitute half the world's population, perform nearly two-thirds of its work hours, receive one-tenth of the world's income and own less than one-hundredth of the world's property.

United Nations Report 1980

Tell me why do babies starve when there's enough food to feed the world? Why, when there's so many of us are there people still alone? Why is a woman still not safe when she's in her home?

Tracy Chapman Contemporary

Inspiration

To inspire is to draw air into the lungs - to be inspiring is to breathe life and dreams and have them become real.

Carmen Silva, 1983

Inspiration comes very slowly and quietly.

Brenda Ueland Contemporary

Irony

Some of us are becoming the men we wanted to marry

Gloria Steinem Contemporary

When one has been threatened with a great injustice, one accepts a smaller as a favour.

Jane Welsh Carlyle 19th Century

The King has been very good to me. He promoted me from a simple maid to be a marchioness. Then he raised me to be a queen. Now he will raise me to be a martyr.

Anne Boleyn 16th Century

K

Knowledge

A woman, especially if she have the misfortune of knowing anything, should conceal it as well as she can.

Jane Austen 18th Century

That is what learning is. You suddenly understand something you've understood all your life, but in a new way.

Doris Lessing Contemporary

A man thinks he knows, but a woman knows better.

Chinese Proverb

Women know a lot of things they don't read in the newspapers. It's pretty funny sometimes, how women know a lot of things and nobody can figure out how they know them.

Meridel Le Sueur 20th Century

L

Labels

I have not labeled myself yet. I would
like to call myself revolutionary, for I
am always changing, and growing, it is
hoped for the good of more black
people. I do call myself black when it
seems necessary to call myself anything.

Alice Walker Contemporary

Who, me confused? Not so. Only your
labels split me.

Gloria Anzaldua Contemporary

Ethnic minority? Which one fits me?
Which one encompasses my reality?
And then next year what will the label
be? Enough! I'm stopping. Setting
myself free. No more label-fitting or

fighting for me. Neither am I searching
for tigers or jungles any more - just
beginning to roar.

Leena Dhingra Contemporary

You might think of yourself as just a
person, but when you step out of your
door you know that you will be looked
at by people as just an Asian woman - a
black woman.

Amrit Wilson Contemporary

Living

You must not think that I feel, in spite of
it having ended in such defeat, that my
'life has been wasted' here, or that I
would exchange it with that of anyone I
know.

Isak Dinesen 20th Century

If I had my life to live again, I'd make
the same mistakes, only sooner.

Tallulah Bankhead 19/20th Century

Life is a slate where all our sins are written; from time to time we rub the sponge of repentance over it so we can begin sinning again.

George Sand (Amandine Aurore Lucie Dupin)
19th Century

I don't want to get to the end of my life and find that I just lived the length of it. I want to have lived the width of it as well.

Diane Ackerman Contemporary

Be wicked, be brave, be drunk, be reckless, be dissolute, be despotic, be an anarchist, be a suffragette, be anything you like - but for pity's sake be it to the top of your bent.

Violet Trefusis, Letter to Vita Sackville-West
19/20th Century

What a wonderful life I've had! I only wish I'd realised it sooner.

Colette 19/20th Century

People do not live nowadays. They get about 10% out of life.

Isadora Duncan 19/20th Century

I enjoy life because I am endlessly interested in people and their growth. My interest leads me continually to widen my knowledge of people, and this in turn compels me to believe that the normal human heart is born good. That is it is born sensitive and feeling, eager to be approved and to approve, hungry for simple happiness, and the chance to live. If through circumstance it is overcome with evil, it never becomes entirely evil. There remain in it elements of good, though recessive, which continue to hold the possibility of restoration.

Pearl S Buck 20th Century

Loneliness

Loneliness and the feeling of being unwanted is the most terrible poverty.

Mother Teresa Contemporary

You can get lonesome - being that busy.

Isabel Lennart 20th Century

If I am such a legend, then why am I so lonely?

Judy Garland 20th Century

Love

All the privilege I claim for my own sex [...] is that of loving longest, when existence or hope is gone.

Jane Austen 18th Century

It seems to me that he has never loved, that he has only imagined that he has loved, that there is no real love on his part. I even think that he is incapable of love. He is too much occupied with other thoughts and ideas to become strongly attached to anyone earthly.

Anna Dostoevsky 19th Century

Love is like quicksilver in the hand. Leave the fingers open and it stays. Clutch it, and it darts away.

Dorothy Parker 20th Century

Love must not crush the woman's individuality, nor bind her wings. If love begins to ensnare her, she must make herself free. She must step over all love tragedies and go her own way.

Alexandra Kollontai 20th Century

Him that I love, I wish to be
Free -
Even from me.

Anne Morrow Lindberg 20th Century

Give me a dozen such heartbreaks if that would help me lose a couple of pounds.

Colette 20th Century

I wish I'd a knowed more people. I would of loved 'em all. If I'd a knowed more, I woulda loved more.

Toni Morrison Contemporary

Love is a great beautifier.

Louisa May Alcott 19th Century

The sun's gone dim, and
The moon's turned black;
For I loved him, and
He didn't love back.

Dorothy Parker 20th Century

Loving allows us to live and through living we grow in loving.

Evelyn Mandel Contemporary

I have learned not to worry about love;
but to honor its coming
with all my heart.

Alice Walker Contemporary

When a woman loves another woman, it
brings no shame to her father's
head and no swelling to her own belly.

Saudi Arabian Proverb

Luck

Why is it no one ever sent me yet
One perfect limousine, do you suppose?
Ah no, it's always just my luck to get
one perfect rose.

Dorothy Parker 20th Century

M

Marriage

Marriage is a great institution but I'm not ready for an institution yet.

Mae West 20th Century

I would rather be a beggar and single than a queen and married.

Queen Elizabeth I 16th Century

On the surface, it looks like very hard luck when a woman falls in love with the 'wrong man'. Yet in my case this apparent hard luck may be linked to that strong adolescent premonition about never marrying. Perhaps we unconsciously avoid situations for which we are ill-equipped, even if avoiding them entails an amount of immediate suffering.

Dervla Murphy Contemporary

The Moslem law allows a man to have four wives at the same time. And although it be a thousand times over no sin according to the Moslem law and doctrine, I shall forever call it a sin [...] Everything for the man, and nothing for the woman, is our law and custom. Do you understand now the deep aversion I have for marriage? I would do the humblest work, thankfully and joyfully, if by it I could be independent.

Raden Adjeng Kartini 19th Century

Marriage could be the greatest success in the sociological history of humanity if the man would or could play fair. But, I believe any woman with independent instincts, with the dream of making her individual personality count for something in the world, might just as well shun marriage.

Maud Gonne 19/20th Century

As a married woman, you simply do not have the same relationship with society as an unmarried woman. I believe that marriage is dangerous for a woman.

Simone de Beauvoir 20th Century

I married beneath me. All women do.

Nancy Astor 20th Century

Oh, what a pother, she thought, women make about marriage! And yet who can blame them, when the marriage - and its consequences - is the only thing that women have to make a pother about in their whole lives? [...] Safeguarded, kept in the dark, hinted at, segregated, repressed, all so that at a given moment they may be delivered or may deliver their daughters over, to minister to a man?

Vita Sackville-West 20th Century

I have three pets at home which answer the same purpose as a husband: I have a dog which growls every morning, a parrot which swears all afternoon, and a cat that comes home late at night.

Marie Corelli 19th Century

Happiness in marriage is entirely a matter of chance.

Jane Austen 18th Century

So that ends my first experience of matrimony, which I always thought a highly over-rated performance.

Isadora Duncan 19/20th Century

Memories

Once I was coming down a street in Beverly Hills and I saw a Cadillac about a block long, and out of the side window was a wonderfully slinky mink, and an arm, and at the end of the arm a hand in a white suede glove wrinkled at the wrist, and in the hand was a bagel with a bite out of it.

Dorothy Parker 20th Century

Men

Adam was a rough draft.

Anonymous Contemporary

Some of my best leading men have been horses and gods.

Elizabeth Taylor Contemporary

Macho does not prove mucho.

Zsa Zsa Gabor Contemporary

None of the fifteen legal men, comprising judge, senior and junior barristers and solicitors had ever witnessed childbirth. 'Is it possible,' the judge was to ask 'for a woman to give birth standing up?' Women have given birth under water, in aeroplanes, in comas, lying unnaturally flat on their backs in hospital beds and even after death, but this man wondered if they could do it standing up ...

Nell McCafferty Contemporary

I require only three things in a man: he must be handsome, ruthless and stupid.

Dorothy Parker 20th Century

One cannot be always laughing at a man without now and then stumbling on something witty.

Jane Austen 18th Century

Never accept rides from strange men, and remember that all men are as strange as hell.

Robin Morgan Contemporary

Women want mediocre men, and men are working to be as mediocre as possible.

Margaret Mead 20th Century

You never really know a man until you've divorced him.

Zsa Zsa Gabor Contemporary

Never trust a husband too far, nor a
bachelor too near.

Dorothy Parker 20th Century

Of course I am shocked by his death.
But not nearly as shocked as when he
walked out on me.

Sophie Levene, on hearing of Lord George
Brown's demise.

Money

Somebody almost walked off wid alla
my stuff.

Ntozake Shange Contemporary

Riches do not always score,
Loving words are better far.
Just one helpful act is more
Than a gaudy motor car.
Happy thoughts contentment bring
Crabbed millionaires can't know;
Money doesn't mean a thing -
Try to tell the butcher so!

Dorothy Parker 20th Century

Wealth without virtue
        is a harmful companion
but a mixture of both,
        the happiest friendship.
Sappho 6th Century BC

It takes nothing more than addition,
subtraction and a gift for deceit to
balance a checkbook.
Kendall Hailey Contemporary

The two most beautiful words in the
English language are 'check enclosed'.
Dorothy Parker 20th Century

There will never be enough money
when you follow what is right.
Phyllis Carter Contemporary

I do want to get rich but I never want to
do what there is to do to get rich.
Gertrude Stein 19/20th Century

Some people are more turned on by money than they are by love. In one respect they're alike. They're both wonderful as long as they last.

Abigail Van Buren 20th Century

Woman will always be dependent until she holds a purse of her own.

Elizabeth Cady Stanton 19th Century

I've been rich and I've been poor - rich is better.

Sophie Tucker 19/20th Century

There are dozens of ways of failing to make money. It is one thing to fail to make money because your single talent happens to be a flair amounting to genius for translating the plays of Aristophanes. It is quite another thing to fail to make money because you are black, or a child, or a woman.

Margaret Halsey Contemporary

The only thing I like about rich people is their money.

Nancy Astor 19/20th Century

The money is always there, but the pockets change; it is not in the same pockets after a change, and that is all there is to say about money.

Gertrude Stein 19/20th Century

Morality

When I'm good I'm very good, but when I'm bad I'm better.

Mae West 20th Century

I cannot and will not cut my conscience to fit this year's fashions.

Lillian Hellman 20th Century

I am pure as the driven slush.

Tallulah Bankhead 20th Century

Love is moral even without legal marriage, but marriage is immoral without love.

Ellen Key 19/20th Century

Motherhood

Motherhood is the most emotional experience of one's life. One joins a kind of women's mafia.

Janet Suzman Contemporary

I'm not against mothers. I am against the ideology which expects every woman to have children, and I'm against the circumstances under which mothers have to have their children.

Simone de Beauvoir 20th Century

To marry and have a child, how banal! But to be pregnant without the help of a husband, what merit.

Ho Xuan Huong 19th Century

It is neither necessary nor just to make it imperative on women that they should either be mothers or nothing, or that if they have been mothers they should be nothing else during the whole remainder of their lives.

Harriet Taylor 19th Century

Devoted grandmother though I am now, I strongly resent the assumption that our capacity for childbearing and our natural inclination towards childcare and child-rearing are the only reasons for our being here on Earth.

Mary Stott Contemporary

Mothers and Daughters

My mother was a brilliant person. She came second to nobody. She was the rock of the family [...] She would never, never, never give up.

Corine Lytle Cannon Contemporary

In search of my mother's garden I found my own.

Alice Walker Contemporary

When you came into the world I suffered for three days and two nights. But I have never regarded that as suffering. They say that children like you who have been carried so high in the womb and have taken so long to come down to the daylight are always the children that are most loved, because they have lain so near the mother's heart and have been so unwilling to leave her.

Sidonie Goudeket to her daughter, Colette, 19/20th Century

I have so much I can teach her and pull out of her. I would say you might encounter defeats but you must never be defeated. I would teach her to love a lot. Laugh a lot at the silliest things and be very serious. I would teach her to love life, I could do that.

Maya Angelou Contemporary

Music

When I was growing up in the 1960s, that part of Ireland [County Sligo] was very rural and a lot of the social life took place in people's houses. My mother's cousin was a really nice fiddle player and there were other women who played. There were winters when there used to be a spate of parties [...] We were encouraged to play as children and we were battering away at tin whistles at an early age. I grew up in that kind of environment, where music was very prominent, and I consider it a rich part of my background.

Brid Boland Contemporary

Singing in the church choir was moving, exhilarating, beautiful. [...] Now the Gospel Chorus, that was the choir that sang from the knowledge, the life of the soul. These older women with the sure-footed step and uplifted shoulders carried us through the history and out of the pain to that far-flung freedom so impossible to attain on the streets of the everyday. With shouting and humming, swaying to a music beyond the hearing, they improvised a life of before and a life to attain. This free music was the one to stir me, to stay.

Sandi Russell Contemporary

N

Nationality

As a woman I have no country, as a woman I want no country. As a woman my country is the whole world.

Virginia Woolf 20th Century

Women are all one nation.

Turkish Proverb

When I am abroad I have my two feet firmly planted in Northern Ireland.

Betty Williams Contemporary

America is my country, and Paris is my home town, and it is as it has come to be. After all, anybody is as their land and air is. Anybody is as the sky is low or high, the air heavy or clear, and anybody is as there is wind or no wind there. It is that which makes them and the arts they make and the work they do and the way they eat and the way they drink and the way they learn and everything. And so I am an American and I have lived half my life in Paris, not the half that made me, but the half in which I made what I made.

Gertrude Stein 19/20th Century

In the London Clubs, literary and social, I always held my peace, a difficult task for any woman, but one requiring superhuman effort in an Irishwoman.

Daisy Bates 19/20th Century

The longer I live the more I turn to New Zealand. I thank God I was born in New Zealand. A young country is a real heritage, though it takes one time to recognise it. But New Zealand is in my very bones.

Katherine Mansfield 20th Century

O

Opportunity

Too often, the opportunity knocks, but
by the time you push back the chain,
push back the bolt, unhook the two
locks and shut off the burglar alarm, it's
too late.

Rita Coolidge Contemporary

One doesn't recognise in one's life the
really important moment - not until it's
too late.

Agatha Christie 20th Century

Oppression

The white man has raped the black
man's culture and used it as a machine
to oppress him. He told me that what I
venerate most was backward and
barbaric, referring to our grandfathers,
our great warriors, our generals - to

Chaka, to Makana and all those - as barbarians! Because in order to destroy me as a proud human being with that black dignity, he had to destroy my identity from the core of my culture.

Winnie Mandela Contemporary

Accepting the rights of those with superior force to dominate those who are weaker, whether man over woman or western nation over Asian nation, is an argument for savagery, not civilisation.

Kishida Toshiko 19th Century

It was heartening to hear that the World Press at least realised that Zia was still the deplorable murderer he had always been, and continued in office only with the patronage of outside powers. Still, it was a shock to read in the newspaper that after a tour of Afghan refugee camps, Margaret Thatcher presented Zia with a Certificate declaring him 'The last bastion of the free world'.

Benazir Bhutto Contemporary

P

Pain and Suffering

Pain is the root of knowledge.

Simone Weil 20th Century

The pain of love is the pain of being alive. It's a perpetual wound.

Maureen Duffy Contemporary

Flowers grow out of dark moments.

Corita Kent Contemporary

It is the unknown of the black pit of suffering that breeds fear, and makes people run away from their own suffering and deny the suffering of others.

Nicolette Devas 20th Century

Patriarchy

Patriarchal poetry is the same as
Patriotic poetry is the same as
patriarchal poetry is the same as
Patriotic poetry is the same as
patriarchal poetry is the same.
Patriarchal poetry is the same.

Gertrude Stein 19/20th Century

Patriarchy is the power of the fathers
[...] under patriarchy I live under the
power of the fathers, and I have access
only to so much privilege or influence as
the patriarch is willing to accede to me,
and only for so long as I will pay the
price for male approval.

Adrienne Rich Contemporary

Women must learn not to be subservient
to the wishes of their fathers, husbands
and partners, because then they do not
fulfill their own ambitions.

Petra Kelly Contemporary

Our society, like all other historic civilisations, is a patriarchy. The fact is evident at once if one recalls that the military, industry, technology, universities, science, political office, and finance, in short - every avenue of power within the society, including the coercive force of the police, is entirely in male hands.

Kate Millet Contemporary

Peace and War

Women will always fear war more than men because they are mothers. A woman will always have a baby, her own or her children's, in her arms. She will always be tormented by fear for her children, the fear that one day she might be a witness to their own deaths.

Natalya Baranskaya Contemporary

I am here to relate the injustice of the present [Vietnam] war to the injustice of poverty and racism at home. The two problems are inextricably bound together.

Coretta King Contemporary

They tell you that you bear none of the burdens of war. It is one of the great arguments brought against you when you ask for equal rights with men.

Droits des Femmes 19th Century French
Suffragist Journal

When we pay our army and our navy estimates, let us set down: so much for killing, so much for maiming, so much for making widows and orphans, so much for bringing famine upon a district, so much for corrupting citizens and subjects into spies and traitors [...] so much for letting loose the daemons of fury rapine and lust within the fold of cultivated society [...] We shall by this means know what we have paid our money for, whether we have made a good bargain.

Anna Laetitia Barbauld 18th Century

When I finally reached England I was paralysed by conflicting emotions: private duty, public disgust and a longing to forget both and join those suffering the war. It is hard to stay on the outside and watch what you can neither help nor change. It is far easier to close your eyes and your mind and jump into the general misery, where you have almost no choices left, but a lot of splendid company.

Martha Gellhorn 20th Century

I could not give my name to aid the slaughter in this war, fought on both sides for grossly material ends, which did not justify the sacrifice of a single mother's son. Clearly, I must continue to oppose it, and expose it, to all whom I could reach with voice or pen.

Sylvia Pankhurst 19/20th Century

Arise, all women who have hearts,
whether your baptism be that of water
or tears! Say firmly "We will not have
great questions decided by irrelevant
agencies [...] We, women of one country,
will be too tender of those of another
country to allow our sons to be trained
to injure theirs.

Julia Ward Howe 19th Century

Pleasure

When I am writing, I allow myself small
ritualised pleasures as breaks from the
writing-pleasures. The cup of herbal tea,
bright light, luxury of the fan heater for
half an hour. Tidying the workplace,
because that's part of the work. A few
minutes stretching or dancing, because
the body is part of it.

Helen McNeil Contemporary

Only in the snow can both sexagenarian
and child squat on the same small
sledges and abandon themselves to the

slopes. They feel alike and exchange smiles [...] Oh simple, precarious, eternal realm of snow! You have created this indulgence - the duty to amuse oneself, the right to live in the body which, from every hour devoted to you enhances in perfection, pulsing with new strength at every fall.

Colette 20th Century

You wear yourself out in the pursuit of wealth or love or freedom, you do everything to gain some right, and once it's gained, you take no pleasure in it.

Oriana Fallaci Contemporary

When I feel physically as if the top of my head were taken off, I know that is poetry.

Emily Dickinson 19th Century

The colour purple is a metaphor for the treasures the world has to offer, including love and sexual enjoyment between women.

Alice Walker Contemporary

Too much of a good thing can be wonderful.

Mae West 20th Century

Potential

I'm not going to limit myself just because people won't accept the fact that I can do something else.

Dolly Parton Contemporary

I'm disturbed by the fact that black women are making a tremendous contribution in their communities in this country - and there seems to be a vendetta to stifle this, to blot it out; the men, somewhere, are not playing a fair game. They don't give the black women an opportunity to honestly realise their

potential and to recognise that potential
when it does come forth.

Ellen Khuzwayo Contemporary

When nothing is sure, everything is
possible.

Margaret Drabble Contemporary

Poverty

In this country [USA], lesbianism is a
poverty - as is being brown, as is being a
woman, as is being just plain poor.

Cherrié Moraga Contemporary

While for a man, poverty means
starvation, for a woman it invariably
also involves rape and a myriad of
forms of sexual exploitation.

Manushi Collective Contemporary

A survival existence on or just below the breadline is not a full life. And all women are entitled to that.

Mary Daly (Ireland) Contemporary

Single women have a dreadful propensity to being poor.

Jane Austen 18th Century

Power

Everybody in the world was in a position to give them [black girls] orders. White women said 'Do this'. White children said 'Give me that'. White men said 'Come here'. Black men said 'Lay down'.

Toni Morrison Contemporary

We are people at the bottom of the mountain struggling to go up and saying to those in power who are at the top: 'Come down, meet us halfway so that we can live and share and be together.' And the longer they delay coming down [...] well, we are coming up, and the harder they will fall when they finally tumble down.

Motlalepula Chabaku Contemporary

I am a woman in the prime of life, with certain powers and those powers severely limited by authorities whose faces I rarely see.

Adrienne Rich Contemporary

Present

The present enshrines the past.

Simone de Beauvoir 20th Century

Progress

I was taught that the way of progress is neither swift nor easy.

Marie Curie 19/20th Century

Questions

The shortest answer is doing.

English Proverb

For too long women have sat down, looked at themselves, maybe accepted certain things as the way of life; but they've stopped and said: 'What is happening? Who am I? Who are we? Where do we come from?' And I think this embodies the 'why' women have taken the stand they have taken - they are beginning to realise their potential.

Ellen Khuzwayo Contemporary

There is really nothing more to say -
except why. But since why is difficult to
handle, one must take refuge in how.

Toni Morrison Contemporary

I believe any woman for whom the
feminist breaking of silence has been a
transforming force can also look back to
a time when the faint, improbable
outlines of unaskable questions, curling
in her brain cells, triggered a shock of
recognition at certain lines, phrases,
images, in the work of this or that
woman, long dead, whose life and
experience she could only dimly try to
imagine.

Adrienne Rich Contemporary

How do you like what you have? This is
a question that anybody can ask
anybody. Ask it.

Gertrude Stein 20th Century

The best stories are those that ask a question: what will happen to her? Will they fall in love and live happily ever after? Whodunnit? And the question that I wrote *Benefits* to examine (though perhaps not answer) was this: What would actually happen to you, me and the woman next door, if the British Government introduced a wage for mothers? Inevitably, because I didn't want to avoid the challenge of asking how such a thing might come to be, in what circumstances might a British Government do it?

Zoë Fairbairns Contemporary

R

Recovery

Out of every crisis comes the chance to
be reborn, to reconceive ourselves as
individuals, to choose the kind of
change that will help us to grow and to
fulfil ourselves more completely.

Nena O'Neill Contemporary

Recovery is a process, not an event.

Anne Wilson Schaef Contemporary

Regret

Make it a rule of life never to regret and
never look back. Regret is an appalling
waste of energy; you can't build on it; it
is good only for wallowing in.

Katherine Mansfield 20th Century

Religion

If there had been no priesthood the world would have advanced ten thousand times better than it has now.

Annandabai Joshee 19th Century

I often ask myself uneasily: is religion indeed a blessing to mankind? Religion, which is meant to save us from our sins, how many sins are committed in thy name?

Raden Adjeng Kartini 19th Century

Reputation

Until you've lost your reputation you never realise what a burden it is, or what freedom really is.

Margaret Mitchell 20th Century

Miss Frances Wright was known by name and reputation to almost everyone. The outrageous nature of her experimental colony and the scandals that had come out of it had made her a general subject of gossip [...] as a result, almost everyone planned to attend her lecture, see her in person, and be scandalised.

Fanny Trollope 19th Century

Resistance and Struggle

What are our reasons for publishing *Sekai Fujin* [Women of the World]? [...] I see that as far as women are concerned virtually everything is coercive and oppressive, making it imperative that women rise up and forcefully develop our own social movement. This truly is an endless enterprise [...]

Fukuda Hideko 19/20th Century

I feel like I'm fighting a battle when I didn't start a war.

Dolly Parton Contemporary

At fifteen life had taught me undeniably
that surrender, in its place, was as
honourable as resistance, especially if
one had no choice.

Maya Angelou Contemporary

When the struggle was over [Telangana
uprising] they decided that the
unmarried women should go and
marry, the married ones should go back
to their families and the men should
study law. We didn't have a say at all.
Till then we never thought of families or
children or of holding on to them!

Mallu Swarajyam Contemporary

The English may batter us to pieces but
they will never succeed in breaking our
spirit.

Maud Gonne 19/20th Century

Women must get educated and strive
for their own independence, they can't
just go on asking the men for everything. The young intellectuals are all

chanting 'Revolution! Revolution!' but I say the revolution will have to start in our homes, by achieving equal rights for women.

Jiu Jin 19th Century

When I hear men carrying on interminably about female chastity I burst out laughing [...] Where do all of these debauched men get the right to emphasise chastity? Rise up, women! Wake up! We women must struggle not only against husbands, but against the entire self-serving world of men [...] Our demands for freedom and equality with men will not be won easily just because we will it; they will not be won if we do not raise our voices, if no blood is shed.

Kanno Suga 19th Century

I am going to die and I wish all the sisters who remain will continue the struggle until the revolution succeeds and women gain equal rights with men.

Nguyen Thi Nghia 20th Century

One of the principal tasks of the Revolution in China is the emancipation of over 200 million women from the bondage of semi-feudal and medieval social ideas and customs. As long as this great human mass is not liberated, a real revolutionary change, not only in the institutions of the country, but in the general life and thought of the people will not be effected.

Soong Ching Ling 20th Century

If asked 'Do you have a husband' girls are urged to say 'Yes, his surname is Viet and his given name is Nam'.

Chen Yu-Hsiuy 20th Century

Black women in South Africa live their daily lives within a framework of apparently immutable laws that have said, for hundreds of years, that if you are both black and female you may not aspire, you are not equal and you have no rights. But those who spoke to me so frankly do not accept their status: they are neither passive nor victim. They certainly do not sit with their hands folded listlessly in their laps [...] The shout of "Amandla! Ngawethu!" rings clear, and there are clearly those who are prepared to die so that there may be power to the people in South Africa.

Beata Lipman Contemporary

S

Self-knowledge

I need to take an emotion breath, step
back, and remind myself who's actually
in charge of my life.

Judith M Knowlton Contemporary

There's a period of life when we
swallow a knowledge of ourselves and
it becomes either good or sour inside.

Pearl Bailey 20th Century

Men look at themselves in mirrors.
Women look for themselves.

Elissa Melamed Contemporary

You say I am mysterious
Let me explain myself
In a land of oranges
I am faithful to apples.

Elsa Gidlow Contemporary

My Guru gave me but one precept
'From without withdraw your gaze
within
And fix it on the Inmost Self'.
Taking to heart this one precept
Naked I began to roam.

Lal Ved 14th Century

Self-worth

The recognition of self as valuable for
being what it is can be a strong basis for
solidarity among the oppressed whether
black in a white society, female in a
male-dominated society or Muslim in a
Hindu society.

Dvaki Jain Contemporary

Painting changed me. Instead of feeling a hopeless muddle, inadequate in any given situation, doomed to be a misfit, an urgent purpose gave me direction. Using paint as a medium of transport, as it were, I had found a way to cast out my inner confusion.

Nicolette Devas 20th Century

Don't compromise yourself. You're all you've got.

Janice Joplin 20th Century

No one can make you feel inferior without your consent.

Eleanor Roosevelt 19/20th Century

Women who set a low value on themselves make life hard for all women.

Nellie McClung Contemporary

Senses

The language of touch, so well-known to lovers and aggressors, remains through life a means of communication infinitely varied and capable of great subtlety. ..at the beginning and end of life it is through touch predominantly that feelings are expressed - towards the very young and the very old.

Elinor Goldschmied Contemporary

Make the most of every sense: glory in all the facets of pleasure and beauty which the world reveals to you through the several means of contact which nature provides. But of all the senses, sight must be the most delightful.

Helen Keller 20th Century

Sex

It is depressing to have to insist that sex is not an unnecessary, morally dubious self-indulgence but a basic human need, no less for women than for men.

Ellen Willis Contemporary

If sex is such a natural phenomenon, how come there are so many books on how to?

Bette Midler Contemporary

In fact, it's quite ridiculous, the shapes people throw when they get down to it. There are few positions more ridiculous - to look at - than the positions people adopt when they are together. Limbs everywhere. Orifices gaping. Mucus pouring out and in. Sweat flying. Sheets wrecked. Animals and insects fleeing the scene when the going gets rough. Noise? My dear, the evacuation of Dunkirk in World War Two was an intellectual discussion compared to it. Once in a while, of course, there's silence. Usually afterwards. It's called exhaustion.

Nell McCafferty Contemporary

It's pitch, sex is. Once you touch it, it clings to you.

Margery Allingham 20th Century

The Crusaders, we are told, put their wives into chastity belts before they sailed off for the Holy Land. They did not, for certain, put their own sexual equipment out of action for the duration.

Mary Stott Contemporary

I had a feeling that Pandora's box contained the mysteries of women's sensuality, so different from man's, and for which man's language was inadequate. The language of sex had yet to be invented. The language of the senses was yet to be explored. Although women's attitude to sex was quite different from that of men, we had not yet learned to write about it.

Anaïs Nin 20th Century

Sexuality
Basically, heterosexuality means men first. That's what it's all about.

Charlotte Bunch Contemporary

The idea should be the capacity to love a woman as well as a man, one or the other, a human being, without feeling fear or constraint or obligation.

Simone de Beauvoir 20th Century

I, for one, identify a woman as a lesbian who says she is.

Cheryl Clarke Contemporary

The subject of lesbianism
is very ordinary; it's the question
of male domination that makes
everybody angry.

Judy Grahn Contemporary

Female sexuality has been seen essentially as a response to male sexuality and intercourse. There has rarely been any aknowledgement that female sexuality might have a complex nature of its own which would be more than just the logical counterpart of [what we think of as] male sexuality.

Shere Hite Contemporary

Sisterhood

Sisterhood, like female friendship, has at its core the affirmation of freedom.

Mary Daly 19/20th Century

I have an immeasurable desire that women should sigh in sympathy.

Virginia Woolf 20th Century

What we suffragettes aspire to be when we are enfranchised is ambassadors of freedom to women in other parts of the world, who are not so free as we are.

Christabel Pankhurst 19/20th Century

Sisterhood is Powerful
Sisterhood is Global

Robin Morgan Contemporary

Success

Success to me is having ten honeydew melons and eating only the top half of each.

Barbra Streisand Contemporary

Integrity is so perishable in the summer months of success.

Vanessa Redgrave Contemporary

I've got two reasons for success and I'm standing on both of them.

Betty Grable 20th Century

If you're small, you better be a winner.

Billie Jean King Contemporary

Success is counted sweetest by those who ne'er succeed.

Emily Dickinson 19th Century

Survival

The love expressed between women is particular and powerful, because we have had to love in order to live; love has been our survival.

Audre Lord Contemporary

See
No matter what you have done
I am still here,
And it has made me dangerous, and
wise.
And brother,
You cannot whore, perfume and
suppress me any more.
I have my own business in this skin
And on this planet.

Gail Murray 1970

In prison I found my heart open to love
- how I do not know - as if I were back
in early adolescence. In prison I
remembered how I had burst out
laughing as a child, while the taste of
tears from the harshest and hardest days
of my life returned to my mouth.

Nawal el Sa'adawi Contemporary

A black woman faces a three-fold disability in this country: she has to overcome the disadvantage of being black, the disadvantage of being a woman, and the disadvantage of her African cultural background in an essentially westernised environment.

Winnie Mandela Contemporary

All women hustle. Women watch faces, voices, gesture, moods. The person who has to survive through cunning.

Marge Piercy Contemporary

Surviving means being born over and over.

Erica Jong Contemporary

T

Talent

I believe talent is like electricity. We do not understand electricity. We use it. Electricity makes no judgement. You can plug into it, and light up a lamp, keep a heart pump going, light a cathedral, or you can electrocute a person with it [...] I think talent is like that. I believe every person is born with talent.

Maya Angelou Contemporary

Thought

Your mind is a tool for you to use in any way you wish. The thoughts you choose to think create the experiences you have. Do not think your mind is in control. You are in control of your mind. The only thing you ever have any control of is your current thought. Your old thoughts have gone, there is nothing you can do about them except live out the experiences they caused. Your future thoughts have not been formed, and you do not know what they will be. Your current thought, the one you are thinking right now, is totally under your control.

Louise L Hay Contemporary

Time

I'm working so hard on my time management that I don't get anything done.

Anonymous

There is a time for work. And a time for love. That leaves no other time.

Coco Chanel 19/20th Century

Tranquillity

You will find that deep place of silence right in your room, your garden or even your bathtub.

Elizabeth Kübler-Ross Contemporary

Like water which can clearly mirror the sky and the trees only so long as its surface is undisturbed, the mind can only reflect the true image of the Self when it is tranquil and wholly relaxed.

Indira Deviv 20th Century

Sorrow is tranquillity remembered in emotion.

Dorothy Parker 20th Century

Travel

[Australia is a] prehistoric country in which the knowledge of the 20th Century finds itself at sea.

Daisy Bates 19/20th Century

When she wrote of her life in America, Fanny apologised for saying so much concerning her difficulties with domestic help, but she felt they were characteristic of America and so must be included, along with spitting and other disagreeable topics.

Johanna Johnston, of Fanny Trollope 19th Century

Contrary to popular belief, English women do not wear tweed nightgowns.

Hermione Gingold 20th Century

Too often travel, instead of broadening the mind, merely lengthens the conversation.

Elizabeth Drew 20th Century

We came over here [Europe] to find culture, and if this is it I'll not take a second helping.

Djuna Barnes 20th Century

Truth

If truth is beauty, how come no one has their hair done in the library?

Lily Tomlin Contemporary

When a woman tells the truth she is creating the possibility for more truth around her.

Adrienne Rich Contemporary

Truth is so rare it's delightful to tell it.

Emily Dickinson 19th Century

V

Violence

Women defending pornography symbolise the internalisation of male oppression.

Clodagh Corcoran Contemporary

Rape is nothing more or less than a conscious process of intimidation by which all men keep all women in a state of fear.

Susan Brownmiller Contemporary

It is a common saying in South Africa that when you cross the black woman you have struck a rock, and certainly black women in South Africa have been fearless in the fight for their rights. They have endured incredible hardship and brutality in prison, often in solitary confinement, and have been frequently tortured, while women political prisoners had no study rights and received no remission of sentence.

Winnie Mandela Contemporary

W

Wisdom

Meeting the wise, all sorrows flee
Bliss pervades the being
Hearing their words wipes out
The pain of birth and death.

Sahjo Bai 17th Century

Yes, I am wise, but it's wisdom full of
pain
Yes, I've paid the price, but look how
much I've gained
I am Wise, I am invinvible, I am
Woman.

Helen Reddy Contemporary

Some of the most esteemed of their
women speak in their councils. When
asked why they suffered the women to

speak they replied 'Some women are wiser than some men'. They had not for many years done anything without the advice of a certain aged and grave woman who was always present at their councils [...] they gave much heed to what she said. This wise queen of Conestoga looked with great favour on the Quakers because they did not come to buy or sell, but came in love and respect to them.

Helen Hunt Jackson 19th Century

By the time your life is finished, you will have learned just enough to begin it well.

Eleanor Marx 19th Century

Womanhood

One is not born a woman, but rather becomes a woman.

Simone de Beauvoir 20th Century

The common woman is as common as
the best of bread and will rise.

Judy Grahn Contemporary

A woman told me that a woman told
her that she saw a woman who saw a
woman who made ale of potatoes.

Irish Proverb

... Throughout our history
You call me Mother.
You ban your belly
And call me Mama
How much longer
Will you learn?
My Motherhood is not my Womanhood
Just another dimension of me
A Woman.

Carole Stewart Contemporary

Womanpower

Women can save civilisation only by the broadest co-operative action, by daring to think, by daring to be themselves.

Harriet Stanton Blatch 19/20th Century

Women and Men

Women are expected to do twice as much as men in half the time and for no credit. Fortunately this isn't difficult.

Charlotte Whitton 20th Century

The cock croweth but the hen delivereth the goods.

Anonymous Contemporary

It is fatal to be a man or a woman pure and simple; one must be a woman manly, or a man womanly.

Virginia Woolf 20th Century

When a lion emerges from the forest, no one bothers to ask whether it is male or female.

Ruth Vanita Contemporary

A woman without a man is like a fish without a bicycle.

Gloria Steinem Contemporary

Being a woman is a terribly difficult task since it consists principally of dealing with men.

Anonymous Contemporary

Men and women, women and men. It will never work.

Erica Jong Contemporary

The reason that husbands and wives do not understand each other is because they belong to a different sex.

Dorothy Dix 19/20th Century

Women read men more truly than men read women. I will prove it in a magazine paper some day when I have time; only it will never be inserted: it will be 'declined with thanks', and left for me at the publishers.

Charlotte Brontë 19th Century

They call us the weaker sex. But men are the weaker sex, and every woman knows why.

Nancy Astor 19/20th Century

Women fail to understand how much men hate them.

Germaine Greer Contemporary

Words and Language

No one sleeps in this room without the dream of a common language.

Adrienne Rich Contemporary

Dear Sirs, man to man, manpower, craftsman, working men, the thinking man, the man in the street, fellow countrymen, the history of mankind, one-man show, man in his wisdom, statesman, forefathers, masterful, masterpiece, old masters, the brotherhood of man, Liberty, Equality, Fraternity, sons of free men, faith of our fathers, god the father, god the son, yours fraternally, amen.
Words fail me.

Stephanie Dowrick Contemporary

When women are supposed to be quiet, a talkative woman is a woman who talks at all.

Dale Spender Contemporary

Lying is done with words and also with silence.

Adrienne Rich Contemporary

A word after a word after a word is
power.

Margaret Atwood Contemporary

This is about words, and how they
move
from mouth to mouth;
Raindrops may oceans make,
Visions worlds alter.

Ruth Vanita Contemporary

Although they are
only breath, words
which I command
are immortal.

Sappho 6th Century

In speech with a man a woman is at a
disadvantage - because they speak
different languages. She may
understand his. Hers he will never
speak nor understand. In pity, or from
other motives, she must therefore,
stammeringly, speak his. He listens and
is flattered and thinks he has her mental

measure when he has not touched even
the fringe of her consciousness.

Dorothy Richardson 19th Century

Language is magic: it makes things
appear and disappear.

Nicole Brossard Contemporary

Work

The best careers advice to give the
young is, find out what you like doing
best and get someone to pay you for
doing it.

Katherine Whilehaen 20th Century

Take your secretary to lunch. He'll
appreciate it.

Anonymous Contemporary

Sometimes the best man for the job isn't.

Anonymous Contemporary

Y

Youth

How absurd and delicious it is to be in love with someone younger than yourself. Everyone should try it.

Barbara Pym 20th Century

Paradoxical as it may seem, to believe in youth is to look backward; to look forward we must believe in age.

Dorothy Parker 20th Century

Your own favourite quotes

Keywords

Author Index

155

THE ATTIC QUIZ BOOK

Gráinne Healy and
Patricia O'Connor

The whackiest, whizziest quizzes ever!
600 questions (and all the answers!) on
every topic (about women!) under the
sun (and some over the moon!)

£2.95 Attic Press
ISBN 0-946211-89-2